MAKING MONEY ONLINE MADE EASY

Anthony Chinedu

All Right Reserved.

No portion of this book may be reproduced in any form without the written permission of the author except brief excerpts in magazine articles; reviews etc. and the source must be mentioned.

ISBN: 9798371707390

For further information write:

Anthony Chinedu

17 Olorunlogbon Street

Anthony Village, Lagos, Nigeria

Tel: +2348036219129,

Email: greatawakeningteam@gmail.com

www.facebook.com/rapturedreadyteam

www.facebook.com/evanganthonyben

TABLE OF CONTENT

HOW TO MAKE MONEY ONLINE 4
LEGIT WAYS TO MAKE MONEY ONLINE 10
HOW TO BECOME A SOCIAL MEDIA MANAGER. 16
HOW TO WRITE FOR SOMEONE ELSE'S WEBSITE OR BLOG. 22
HOW TO GET PAID FOR YOUR CRAFT. 27
HOW TO PROOFREAD DOCUMENTS 31
TAKE SURVEYS AND ANSWER QUESTIONS. 39
SELLING YOUR UNWANTED STUFF ONLINE 44
HOW TO BECOME A VIRTUAL ASSISTANT. 48
HOW TO RENT OUT YOUR CAR PARKING SPACE. 53
HOW TO SELL YOUR HAIR FOR WIGS OR EXTENSIONS 56
HOW TO BECOME A VIRTUAL ASSISTANT. 62
HOW YOU CAN SELL YOUR USED BOOKS ON AMAZON. 69
HOW TO CREATE A BLOG FOR FREE AND MAKE MONEY FROM IT. 74
HOW TO WRITE AN EBOOK AND SELL IT ONLINE. 82

Chapter 1

HOW TO MAKE MONEY ONLINE

If you're struggling to make ends meet and have the time, energy and desire to earn extra money online, there are many options available. The good news is that this isn't as hard as it may sound! The key is finding something that will enable you to make money from home without having to spend a lot of time at it—and doing so easily. Here are some ideas for how:

Start by setting up a local business and offering your services to others in your area.

Start with a small, local business that you can grow into something bigger. For example, if you live in the city of San Francisco, why not start by selling coffee? You could start by serving coffee at events or tastings around town and then expand on that idea.

Even if you don't want to work for yourself full time right away, there are many ways in which people can earn money online without having their own businesses (or even any employees).

Write an ebook and sell it online.

You can write an ebook and sell it online.

Ebooks are digital versions of books that are sold in the same way as physical copies, except they have no paper or ink to go through. They're much more convenient to read on your phone or computer screen than printed books, so they're perfect for people who don't want to carry around heavy hardbacks with them wherever they go! Ebooks also allow you to make money from home without having any investment into creating what would normally be a costly product (such as printing).

So how do you get started? First off, create a great title for your ebook—something catchy like "How To Make Money Online!" If possible try adding some keywords related specifically towards those terms such as "how" or "make" so that when someone searches through Amazon looking for information about making money online these words will appear at first glance followed by other relevant terms such as "ebook download" etcetera."

Create a blog for free and make money from it.

If you want to make money from your blog, then it's important to start by finding a topic that is of interest and relevance to the readers. To do this, use Google Trends or any other search engine tool available on the internet. Once you've found keywords related to your chosen niche, make sure that they are relevant and not too broad so as not to confuse people who might be looking for something else altogether. For example: if someone searches "how much does it cost per month" they are unlikely going on your blog unless they know exactly what they want!

Once you have decided what type of content will appear on your site then decide whether or not there is demand for such content elsewhere online (i.e., social media). Check out sites like Reddit where users post questions which could be answered by those interested in similar topics but don't necessarily have time themselves learn everything necessary about them -- this could lead them back down another path with us!"

Set up a YouTube channel where you share tutorials, such as how to apply makeup or play music.

You don't need to be a professional videographer or photographer to make money on YouTube. It's easy, and there are a lot of ways you can earn money from your videos—and it doesn't matter if you're a beginner or an expert in the field.

Here are some ideas:

- Make tutorials on how to apply makeup, play music and more.
- Create funny videos that teach people how to do things they didn't know they could do (like making their own ice cream).
- Share information about products that people might not otherwise find through Google search results (for example, if someone searches "how long does it take for solar panels" but all they see is ads for solar panels).

Make money by sharing links on social media around products and services that interest you.

- How to make money by sharing links on social media around products and services that interest you.
- You can find product and service information, then share it on your social media accounts.
- This is a great way to make money online, especially if you have a lot of followers on Facebook or Twitter.

Turn your photography hobby into a money-making opportunity.

You need to be good at photography. You also need a good camera, website or social media page, and the knowledge that you can charge for the time you spend taking photos.

You'll also want to offer services as an online photographer—think wedding photo packages or family portraits plus a few more expensive shots if desired. These are great ways to make more money on top of what your clients pay for their sessions (and potentially even more by charging extra).

Sell your hair for wigs or extensions.

Selling your hair for wigs and extensions is a great way to make money online. If you have long, thick hair, it's likely that someone will want to buy it from you.

If you're considering selling your hair for wigs or extensions, there are three things you'll need:

- A wig maker (or someone who can provide the materials)
- Someone who wants to buy your hair (for example, another woman who has long, thick locks)

There are many ways to earn money online.

There are many ways to earn money online. You can start with something small and build up, or you can make money by selling products and services.

You could even use your skills to make some extra cash!

If you're interested in making money online, there are many ways to do it. You just need to find the right one for you!

Chapter 2

LEGIT WAYS TO MAKE MONEY ONLINE

You're not a complete idiot if you've ever thought, "I could make some extra money on the side." But how do you go about doing it? Well, here are 10 legit ways to make money online.

Become a social media manager.

Social media managers are in high demand, and you can earn up to $80,000 per year with the right skills. The job requires you to have a strong understanding of social media platforms and how they work, as well as an interest in writing compelling content for your clients' accounts. You should also be able to create campaigns that help drive traffic back toward your client's website or blog posts.

To get started as an online freelancer, start by researching companies who hire social media managers and their needs (e.g., hourly rate). Then make sure that you have experience working with clients before applying for positions at those companies—this will show potential employers what kind of person you are!

Write for someone else's website or blog.

Writing for a website is a great way to make money online. You can also write about your experiences and share them with other people who are interested in similar topics. If you're passionate about something, it may be time to monetize that passion by writing about it!

Get paid for your craft.

If you have a craft that you've been working on for a while, it's time to sell it. You can start by selling your handmade products on Etsy and eBay. If that doesn't turn out well, try Amazon or another online retailer as well.

Whatever method of selling your crafts you decide upon, make sure they're worth the effort: if people don't want them, they won't buy them—so don't waste your time trying!

Proofread documents.

Proofreading is an essential skill that can help you earn a good living as well. If you want to work from home, proofreading documents is one job that can be done in your spare time and still earn enough money to live comfortably.

Proofreaders usually work on their own schedules: they have all day or night up to choose when they want to proofread something or not. You may choose to do this for yourself, but there are also companies out there which hire freelance editors who are looking for someone who has some experience in the industry before hiring them full-time.

Take surveys and answer questions.

- Take surveys and answer questions. This can be done from anywhere with internet access, so you don't have to spend all your time at home!
- Get paid for your opinions. If a company is interested in what you think, they'll pay you for it! You can even take surveys while watching TV or on the bus—or even while waiting in line and sitting on the toilet (just kidding).

Sell your stuff.

- Sell your old electronics.
- Sell your old books.
- Sell your old clothes and shoes.
- If you have an expensive car, sell it!

Become a virtual assistant.

As a virtual assistant, you will help people with their administrative tasks. You can work from home and make money by doing this work for others. The best part about being a virtual assistant is that it's flexible, so you don't have to commit to any specific hours or days of the week.

The main benefit of becoming one of these types of workers is that they can earn an income while continuing their education or pursuing hobbies outside working hours. This means they'll be able to spend more time with family and friends instead of working at some high-pressure job every day!

As well as having flexibility in your schedule, there are plenty of other perks associated with being an online worker: no commute costs (and therefore no car payments), unlimited holidays/vacations etc...

Sell your old iPhones, iPads and other electronics on Gazelle.

Gazelle is a trusted company that allows you to sell your old electronics. You can get paid fast, with a check in the mail within 24 hours or even sooner!

Gazelle pays you by check or PayPal (they do not pay through Amazon) and they offer free shipping on orders above $25.

Sell your used books on Amazon.

You can sell your used books on Amazon.

You have access to the largest online marketplace in the world, which means you will be able to reach a much wider audience than if you were selling locally. The best part about selling through Amazon is that there are no fees involved—you just set the price and they pay you within 2 days of receiving and inspecting the book. If someone wants to buy it from you, they'll contact you directly through their email address or phone number; this way, no one else will know who owns that particular email address or phone number!

Rent out your car parking space.

If you have a car and have access to a parking space, it's time to make some money. There are several ways you can choose from, but one of the easiest is selling your parking space online.

When looking for an online marketplace, there are two key factors that determine how many potential customers will be willing to pay for your space: location and price. The location should always be somewhere close by so that people know where they'll be able to find it easily if they need somewhere safe and convenient (and perhaps even convenient enough). Pricing will depend on demand—if there aren't many cars in this area at any given time of day/night then offering lower prices may not attract anyone who needs those spaces most often; conversely if there are lots more cars than usual then prices could rise significantly since no one wants their spaces taken up by someone else's vehicle!

Once you've found an appropriate place with good visibility nearby as well as good lighting conditions (ideally both), here's what happens next: advertise through social media channels like Facebook Groups or Instagram feeds...

Quit your job and sit back on the beach with a cold one (to drink)

You can make money online. It's not a scam and it's not illegal. You don't need to spend any money or pay anyone to make money online, but you do need to work hard and be persistent when looking for ways to make money online.

There are many ways that people make money online today: affiliate marketing, blogging, content writing (blogging), selling products on Amazon and other sites like eBay or Etsy etc...

If you want to learn more about these methods then check out my post here: How to Make Money Online with Blogging Tips & Tricks

Once you have the right mindset for making money online, you're ready to take your first steps. Remember that these are the most legitimate ways to make money online and there are many more out there. If any of these doesn't work for you then feel free to try something else!

Chapter 3

HOW TO BECOME A SOCIAL MEDIA MANAGER.

There's a lot of buzz around becoming a social media manager these days, and it's easy to see why. Social media managers are in high demand and can earn six-figure salaries. But there are some caveats when it comes to becoming one: You need to be willing to work hard—and be skilled at your craft—to succeed as a digital marketer. If this sounds like something you're interested in pursuing, read on for some tips on how to become an effective social media manager!

Tips for becoming a social media manager:

You can learn the basics of social media management through online courses. The course you choose will vary, depending on your interests and experience level. For example, if you have no experience with social media marketing but want to learn how it works, then taking an online course that focuses on basic principles is probably better than taking a more advanced one that only covers specific topics related to managing your own account(s).

While studying for one of these courses may help you get up-to-speed fast, it's important not to rely solely on them as your sole source of information when starting out in this field—you'll still need hands-on experience before moving into management roles at larger companies or agencies.

Learn everything you can about social media.

As a social media manager, you'll have to keep up with the ever-changing landscape of social media. You can do this by taking advantage of all the resources available for learning about your field: books, videos and seminars.

- Books: There are many books on social media management that you can read to learn more about what it takes to be successful in this job. Many will also include tips on how they've managed their own accounts or those of others who work for them.
- Videos: You may not be able to get enough information from reading books alone; if so then consider watching some YouTube videos on how best practices are done by other people in similar positions as yours (and don't forget Google). This way there won't be any excuse why someone else gets

ahead while still trying out different approaches themselves!

Become an influencer yourself.

Becoming an influencer yourself is a great way to build your portfolio and establish your authority. The first step is to begin posting on social media, but it's important that you don't just post something random without any context or purpose. You'll want to create content that's helpful and relevant, so use the platform as an opportunity to educate others while they're still interested in what you have to say.

By posting educational posts on Facebook or Instagram (or both), you can reach new followers who might not otherwise search for information about your industry or company in search engines like Google or Bing—which means those people will be more likely than ever before!

Pay for training or certification.

- Certification is a great way to ensure that your company's social media strategy is well-planned, organized and executed.
- Certified Social Media Strategists (CMS) are professionals who have been trained in how to manage social media campaigns for

businesses. They can help you create content that resonates with customers and drives them back to your website or app.
- There are several certifications available that allow you to become a certified social media manager:
- The American Marketing Association's (AMA) Certified Marketer® Program teaches marketers about marketing research, measurement strategies and tactics so they can use data-driven decision making when developing marketing plans for their companies' products or services; the AMA's Marketing Research Professional (MREP) program provides similar training for those who work in market research departments at organisations such as universities

Build your portfolio by blogging about social media.

Blogging is a great way to show off your social media skills and build your portfolio. You can do this while working full-time, which means it's time efficient.

If you have a blog, use it as a resume or CV (curriculum vitae). It also gives potential employers an idea of what kind of person you are based on the content on the site. If they like what they see, they might want to hire you!

You can use this same idea when posting on social media networks as well; just make sure not to post anything inflammatory or offensive so that no one will think less of them by association with someone who writes something like this.

Contact local businesses and offer to create their social media profiles, or choose a niche and go after a specific market like food trucks or real estate.

As a social media manager, you need to be able to effectively communicate with clients and prospects. One way of doing this is by asking for a portfolio of their work before starting your own account. Also, offer to build a free social media profile for them if you're happy with the results. This shows that you are willing to help others succeed in what they do, even if it doesn't involve working on your own content directly (and remember: don't be afraid of asking for help from other professionals).

Learning how to be a social media manager is not complicated, but it does require some legwork.

Becoming a social media manager is not complicated, but it does require some legwork. There are many different ways to get started with this career field and you don't need to be an expert in all of them. The first step is to learn how your platform works and who your audience is on it. After that, you can start building relationships with influencers and brands who want their content shared through your account or website (if you already have one).

If you're interested in learning more about what makes someone fit into this role—or just getting started yourself—read on!

I hope this article has given you enough information to get started on your own social media journey. As I mentioned above, there are many opportunities out there for those who want careers in the field. Just remember that it takes time and patience before you can start getting paid for your work!

Chapter 4

HOW TO WRITE FOR SOMEONE ELSE'S WEBSITE OR BLOG.

Are you a writer? Do you have a great way with words, but don't know how to get your work published online? Well, you're in luck! I've been writing for over 10 years, and I can help you get started. The first step is understanding what kind of job opportunities might be available to writers who want to write for someone else's website or blog. In this post we'll talk about how to find those jobs in order to get started writing and earning money while doing what you love most: creating things!

Find out what you're allowed to do.

- Ask the editor what they want.
- If there is a style guide, find it. It may be online at the publisher's website or it might be in hard copy form, which you can request from them. If you're working on a freelance basis and don't have access to their site, ask the editor if they'll send you a copy of their style guide so that you can translate it into HTML code and add it as an element on your site (see below).

- Ask if there are any restrictions on what kind of content can be written for this particular blog/website/magazine/whatever else so that no matter how much time has passed since its last update this material won't fall out of date when published again later on down the line...

Put together a writing sample.

Now that you know what to write, it's time to put together a sample. The best way to do this is by writing something yourself first—you'll have the most experience with your own voice and style. You can use the same template as above or make something completely new. But whatever you choose, make sure your writing samples are easy for people who read them to understand and digest in less than 10 seconds (if possible).

You could also consider sharing them on social media channels like Facebook or Twitter so that others can see what kind of content you produce!

Don't be afraid to apply for jobs that pay little or nothing.

You can always find work that pays more later. If you're not willing to take on a gig that pays nothing and learn from the experience, then how are you going to get better?

You will learn a lot from the experience of writing for free. There's no better way than doing it yourself first before trying your hand at other people's websites or blogs.

Don't be afraid to write for free just to get your name out there.

Writing for free can be a great way to get your name out there, as well as build your portfolio and author platform.

It's important to note that this doesn't mean you should write articles just for the sake of it—there's no point in writing an article if nobody will read it. However, if you have something interesting that you think would be useful to someone else (or at least amuses them), then go ahead and send them the article! You never know when they might end up using what they've read in future projects or articles on their website/blog...

Have an excuse ready for why you want the job.

It's important to have an excuse ready for why you want the job. This can be a great way of demonstrating that you're interested in working with them, and it also shows that they have time to teach you how they do things. You should explain what your interests are and where you'd like to see yourself in 2 or 3 years' time, as well as any specific skills or experience that would help them out.

Give examples of things you've done in the past—this will demonstrate some kind of passion for writing, which is always good for getting hired on! You could include links from social media sites like Twitter or Facebook (if applicable) as well as blog posts from previous employers/internships/etcetera (don't worry about being too sloppy with this).

You can write for someone else's website or blog if you follow these steps.

- You need to know what you can write and what you cannot.
- You need to know how long the article needs to be, so that it fits into their website or blog.
- When applying for jobs, always include a cover letter or resume with your application. If the company hires someone based on this alone, they may think that you're not qualified!

You don't need to be a professional writer, but you do need to have some experience. If you have none, then it's time to start writing for yourself. It doesn't matter if your first articles are terrible—as long as they are well-written and cover topics that are relevant in today's world will get more readers over time.

Chapter 5

HOW TO GET PAID FOR YOUR CRAFT.

Getting paid for your craft is no easy feat. It takes a lot of time and effort to create something that people want, but once you have created something that you think has value or interest, there are ways to make money from it. In this article, we'll go over some tips on how to get paid for your craft in as little time as possible without sacrificing quality or integrity.

Get Clear on What You Want to Sell.

You need to get clear on what you want to sell and the location where it will be sold. Once you have that figured out, it's time to figure out how much money and how often you want to make sales. If your goal is $500 per month, but only wants 10% of that amount in profits, then setting up a fixed price shop might not be the best option for you.

The next question is: why do I want my craft? Are there elements about this craft that inspire me or give me joy? Or is there something about this craft that makes me feel like I'm contributing something good into the world (I'm sure there are plenty of people out there who could use some encouragement).

Consider Your Audience.

When you're thinking about how to get paid for your craft, it's important to consider the audience. What are their needs? What do they like? Are there any expectations of what you can provide them with?

Are you selling to a niche audience or a general audience? If you're targeting a niche market, then your products will be more specific and tailored toward their needs. For example, if someone wants something that will help them with their home decorating project but also improve overall well-being by reducing stress levels and anxiety levels (and maybe even make them feel more creative), then this person might benefit from getting some insights into Feng Shui instead of just buying some candles or incense burners from Etsy (which includes both).

How can we best reach our target audiences?

Research the Pricing of Your Competitors.

- Research the Pricing of Your Competitors.
- Look at what other people are selling and consider the quality, time involved in making the work and cost of materials.

- Consider the cost of marketing (if you are selling online). The more expensive your product is to market, the more you need to charge for it if you hope to make money on it. If you have a very specific niche audience who will only buy from your store, then maybe that's not as important—but keep this in mind when pricing things out so that they're priced into line with other similar items on Etsy or elsewhere online!

Make Sure Your Prices are Consistent With Your Target Audience.

- Price your work according to the market
- Consider the cost of materials, labor and time in crafting a product.

If you are selling locally, then this can be a lot more difficult to price. However, if you are selling online or even at craft fairs in cities where there is more competition and less room for bargaining with buyers, then it's important that your prices reflect what others are charging for similar items. If possible, look at what other artists are charging for their crafts before setting yours up on Etsy or any other platform where people can find out about them easily (like Facebook).

Let People Know You Sell Crafts.

The best way to get paid for your craft is by selling it. And the easiest way to sell your artwork is to let people know that you're selling it. This can be as simple as putting up an event page on Facebook or posting about it on Instagram. It doesn't need to be fancy, but it does need to make people want more information!

Once they find out what you're doing and how much you charge for each item, they'll almost certainly want one (or more). That's when sales start rolling in!

If you want to get paid for your craft, you can do it.

If you want to get paid for your craft, there are ways to do it. You can do it if you have the willingness and ability to work hard, learn new skills and persist in your efforts. The only thing that stands between an artist and their dream of getting paid for their work is themselves—they must be willing to spend time learning new things that will improve their craft as well as keep them challenged by whatever it is they're doing every day.

We hope these tips have been helpful in getting you started on your journey toward making money from your craft. Remember, the important thing is to do what feels right for you, and don't feel pressured into doing things that aren't good for your business or yourself. You're going to be giving so much of yourself as it is! But if all goes well, then eventually people will start buying from you because they love what you're selling.

Chapter 6

HOW TO PROOFREAD DOCUMENTS

If you're writing a report, article or even an email, it's important that your document is free of errors. Luckily, there are plenty of ways to ensure this happens. In this post we'll cover how to proofread documents so that they're as error-free as possible before sending them out into the world!

Use a different format.

- Use a different format.
- Use a different font, size, and color.
- Use a different document layout.
- Use a different computer or device (iPad vs laptop).
- Try it at night if possible; this will help you see if there are any errors that can be found in low light conditions due to differences in lighting between noon and midnight hours when reading on your computer screen is easier than reading from paper because you can zoom in on what needs fixing without having to keep turning pages back-and-forth to find the text again after turning them once!

Read the document out loud.

The best way to proofread is to read the document out loud. This allows you to hear yourself when reading, which is an important skill in writing. It also helps you identify if the document is too long or short; if it's too long, it will be hard for someone else who might have access rights on your computer to read through without getting bored by how much information they are missing out on.

The second benefit of reading aloud is that it helps you identify structure problems in your sentences and paragraphs—for example, if several sentences end with commas but none are needed at all (or vice versa).

Watch for errors in grammar and mechanics.

Grammar and mechanics are the "nuts and bolts" of writing, the things that make up how we speak. They refer to nouns, verbs, adjectives, adverbs—the whole language! Some common grammar errors include subject-verb agreement (e.g., I go), pronoun agreement (e.g., you're going), subject-verb tense consistency (e.g., I was going), pronoun case/number/antecedent agreement (e..g..I'm wating for my friend).

Check for awkward wordings and misplaced modifiers.

Proofreading is about more than just spelling and grammar. It's also about checking for awkward wordings, misplaced modifiers and any other words that don't make sense.

Check for any redundancies:

- Make sure you've got the right number of articles in a series (e.g., "he/she" or "his/hers"). If there are too many or not enough, it can throw off your reader's attention and make them feel like they're reading an essay instead of reading a story.
- Also make sure that you're not repeating yourself too much—you may want to use different words but try not to say them twice! This will help keep things organized as well as improve clarity overall by making sure everything flows smoothly together at all times

Make sure your document is complete.

When you're proofreading a document, it's important to make sure that your document is complete. This means checking for all of the important components of the text:

- References are accurate and complete
- Title and abstract are accurate and complete

- Formatting is correct

Check for consistency.

Checking for consistency is a great way to make sure your document is free of typos and grammatical errors, but it also helps you avoid writing something that could be interpreted as offensive or inflammatory. Double-check that all numbers are consistent—for example, if you're using $1 billion instead of 1 billion dollars, note that in the margin next to that sentence so readers can see where exactly the error occurred without having to read through everything else in your document (or worse yet, trying to figure out what the heck was happening). Also check capitalization and punctuation: Is every word capitalized? Are all names spelled correctly? Is there an apostrophe at the end of each contraction ("the girl's mother"?), or does someone just not know what one looks like? Finally, keep an eye out for any other potential mistakes such as incorrect punctuation (it'd be awful if someone wrote "it" instead) or misspelled words ("newspaper".).

Beware of common mistakes that are easy to miss.

As you write, make sure you proofread your document. This is the most important step in making sure your document is error-free because it will catch all of the mistakes that are easy to miss.

- Spelling and grammar: Check for spelling mistakes such as "shouldn't" instead of "shouldn't have" or "subsequent" instead of subsequent. Also check for grammatical errors like wrong word order or sentence structure issues (for example: "I am going to work today." does not need a comma). Finally, make sure there are no typos like missing letters (e.g., "N" instead of "U").
- Formatting: Make sure that every section has its own header with correct capitalization, date formats and numbers/dates used throughout the body text (see examples below).

Double-check all names and titles, especially for proper capitalization.

- Double-check all names and titles, especially for proper capitalization.
- Capitalize the first word of a name, and any other words that are the first in the sentence.
- Capitalize the first word of a title, and any other words that are the first in their sentence.

- Use lowercase for all other words in a name or title (ex: "Mr." should be written as "mister").

Ensure that numbers appear consistently throughout the document, and in a consistent format (for example, either "two" or "2," but not both).

The most important thing you can do to ensure consistency in numbers is to use a consistent style throughout your document. If you have a standard number format, such as "2" or "3," make sure that it appears consistently throughout the document. The same goes for font size and spacing: if you are using Courier New as your default typeface, then stick with that!

If you're unsure whether something needs further attention (such as inconsistent capitalization), ask someone at work who knows more about formatting than yourself—they'll probably be able to help point out potential issues and suggest ways around them. Additionally, check with HR or another manager before posting anything publicly on social media so they can review what's going up there too!

Proofreading is a crucial step before publishing any document!

Proofreading is a crucial step before publishing any document. It helps you catch mistakes and errors, which in turn can save you a lot of time later on. Proofreading also helps make sure your document is consistent across all sections of the text.

It's important not only because it will help prevent embarrassing missteps from being made in front of clients or colleagues, but also because proofreading ensures that every word has been carefully considered for its potential impact on the reader—and therefore, whether or not they want to keep reading further down into what might be an otherwise boring article about something boring like sales tax reform in Georgia (which we're pretty sure never happens).

We hope you found this guide useful in your quest to proofread documents. Remember that there is never a perfect way to do it, and that just because one method works for you doesn't mean it'll work every time. Always test out different strategies before committing them completely!

Chapter 7

TAKE SURVEYS AND ANSWER QUESTIONS.

We're always looking for stories from our readers. If you have any opinions on a particular topic, we'd love to hear them! Here are some questions that we've been asked recently:

What is the first thing you do when you wake up?

This question is about your morning routine. What do you do when you wake up?

- Check your email.
- Check social media accounts for news, events and things that are going on in the world around us.
- Go to the bathroom (or use a washcloth).
- Make sure that everything is ready for the day ahead of me before leaving my bedroom/living room area (I'm not talking about making sure that I have coffee brewing).

What kind of sandwich do you like to get?

- Meat, cheese and bread.
- What kind of meat? Do you like beef or chicken? How about turkey or ham? Do you want it fried in oil or not at all? And what

about the cheese—what kind of cheese do you prefer on your sandwiches: cheddar, Swiss or American (the white kind)? Don't forget about the bread! Is it whole wheat with no additives but still slightly sweetened and soft enough for wrapping around a sandwich filling without being too dry and tough after sitting in your hands for too long during lunchtime rush hour traffic on school days when everyone else is hungry too but doesn't want anything too messy because their parents told them not eat anything until after class ends so they won't get detention if there's any leftover food lying around somewhere else in their house besides where they usually eat breakfast."

What was the last gift you gave someone?

I would say that my wife is one of my best friends and she has always been there for me. We were married almost ten years ago now, so it's been a long time since I've given her anything really meaningful in terms of gifts or anything like that. But what I do know is that every year when we have Christmas dinner at our house with all our family members, she always gets me something special from somewhere else besides just being from where we live—like maybe some kind of candy or something like that that she knows I love!

What was the last gift you got from someone?

What was the last gift you received?

I would like to know what was the last gift you received from someone. How did they make you feel when giving it and how did that make you feel about yourself. Please answer as much detail as possible, including: who gave it to me, where I was when they gave it to me and why they gave me this gift in particular

How many pairs of shoes do you own?

We don't know how many pairs of shoes you own, and we don't care.

We don't have time to count all your shoes. We're busy, and so are you! If you want us to count your shoes on this survey, then write down the number when prompted (and please keep in mind that it's just a number).

Do you think playgrounds should have more or less equipment?

As a playground operator, you should think about how much equipment is needed. There are many different ways to answer this question:

- More equipment means more fun for everyone. With more equipment, children can play games and enjoy the outdoors without worrying about safety or getting hurt. However, more expensive materials may be required for these new structures.
- Less equipment means fewer accidents at the park and less maintenance costs overall because there's less wear on your facilities (and thus less need for repairs). This could also mean that fewer people will visit your park if they don't feel like they have enough room inside—so consider increasing your capacity by adding an additional building or two!

We love hearing from our readers!

We love hearing from our readers! It's a great way to learn about what you like and what we should cover. We want to make sure that the content on this website is as relevant and useful as possible, so it's important for us to hear directly from people who use it.

If there are any questions or comments about the site or our work, please let us know in the comments section below or by emailing us at

We're so excited to see all these surveys! We hope you'll continue to send us your responses and questions, because it's very much encouraged. Thank you so much for reading this far and taking part in our experiment!

Chapter 8

SELLING YOUR UNWANTED STUFF ONLINE

Selling used items online is a great way to find additional revenue. It can also be a good way to clear out some of your clutter and make room for new things—if you're willing to give them away. In this post, we'll take a look at how selling unwanted stuff online works and what you can expect when selling on eBay, Amazon and other sites.

How to identify what to sell.

When you're considering what to sell, take a look around your home. Try to identify every item that is not being used and ask yourself why it isn't being used. If you don't use something, don't buy it—or at least think twice before doing so (and then again).

If there's something in your life that doesn't make sense anymore, maybe now is the right time to get rid of it! Just remember: if someone else would want this item more than they want yours, they probably will pay more money too!

How to determine the best way to sell it.

You can sell your items online in many different ways. The most popular way is through auction websites like eBay, where you list your items and bid on them. eBay has a lot of competition, so you have to be careful to price your items correctly and be sure that they're in good condition before listing them on the site.

If you're looking for an alternative method, there are other options available:

- Craigslist: This free website lets users post ads for free or charge a small fee per post (up to $500 annually). There's no limit on how long an item can stay up for sale there either; however, unlike with other sites listed here where everything has a fixed price tag attached at all times until someone buys it—you'll need some patience if this happens!

What you can actually get for your stuff.

The first thing you need to do is determine the value of your item, which means taking into account both its quality and condition. If it's in good condition, then it has a higher value than if it's in poor condition.

If you don't know how much an item is worth, try using some common sense: Is there any damage?

What about scratches or dents? Does the label still have its original price tag on it? These things can help give an idea of how much money someone might be willing to pay for ownership over something like this!

Once you know what kind of price range we're talking about here (and remember that prices will vary depending on location), go ahead and see what websites sell similar items online—but make sure they're reputable ones before purchasing anything from them!

Unused items can bring in money and make room for new things

If you've got unwanted items that you want to get rid of, there are many ways to make some extra cash. eBay is one of the most popular options for selling items online. You can also sell your stuff on Facebook Marketplace or Craigslist—but if you're looking for a more traditional garage sale, consider holding one from time-to-time as well!

There are many other ways that people have found success selling their unwanted household goods: you might even consider holding an estate sale at home (if this works for your situation). It'll be time consuming and expensive, but it's worth it if the payoff will make up for it all!

We hope this article has given you some ideas on how to get rid of your unwanted items. The internet is a great place for selling all kinds of things, but the key is finding a way that works for you and your lifestyle. We recommend doing some research before diving in, so that it doesn't turn into a full-time job!

Chapter 9

HOW TO BECOME A VIRTUAL ASSISTANT.

If you're looking to make a career change or simply looking for something new, the field of virtual assistants might be right up your alley. Not only are they fast-paced and flexible, but they can also be lucrative.

Intro to being a virtual assistant

What is a virtual assistant?

A virtual assistant is someone who works remotely for an employer, usually in the form of email correspondence. They're not employed by the same company as their client or client's employees — instead, they work from home on a contract basis and report directly to them. These businesses use these services as part of their overall business model because it helps them save money on office space and other overhead costs. The key benefit is that clients don't have to pay for any employee benefits like healthcare coverage or vacation time; instead, all those things are taken care of by the VA themselves (or at least those who have been approved).

How do I become a Virtual Assistant?

There are two main ways you can go about becoming one: either through an agency that specializes in hiring VAs or directly through your existing employer if they offer this type of position as part-time work opportunity within their company structure itself

What can you do?

You can do anything.

You can do anything you want, as long as it's legal and ethical, of course. You may be wondering what your options are and how to decide which path is right for you. That's where we come in! We'll help guide you through the process of choosing a career that is right for YOU—and we'll also show you how to make money doing it!

Marketing yourself

- Do your research. The first thing you need to do is figure out if there are any virtual assistant jobs out there that suit your skills and experience, then go ahead and apply for them.
- Have a website. If you don't already have one, now would be a good time to get one up and running! It's important because it shows potential employers that you can be

trusted with their information, so make sure everything works properly before sending in any applications (and by "everything," I mean everything).
- Use social media platforms such as Twitter and Facebook as well as LinkedIn if possible; these will help build connections within the industry which can lead directly into finding new clients or even getting hired by existing ones!

Dealing with clients

Dealing with clients is the most important part of being a virtual assistant. It's your bread and butter, after all. The good news is that you can handle it!

It's always best to be nice and pleasant with clients, but there are times when they might not be so easy to please—especially if they're difficult or demanding in some way. In those cases (and there will be many), try being professional but also ask yourself how much patience you can afford before snapping back at them. If possible, try not making any snap judgments about their behavior; instead focus on your own behavior instead of getting upset at theirs (which only makes things worse).

There is hope and a bright future in the world of virtual freelance work.

There is no doubt that the world of virtual freelance work has changed, and it will continue to change in the future. In fact, there are many ways you can make money as a virtual assistant. The first step toward becoming one is deciding how much time and energy you want to put into it—and what kind of career path you want for yourself in this new field. Once your goals are set, it's time for action!

If you're a creative, hardworking person who has the desire to help others and make money doing it, virtual assistant work can be an excellent way to bring your dreams into reality. The possibilities are endless—from creating web pages or writing blog posts for your clients to scheduling meetings and managing social media accounts. With so many tasks that need completing on a daily basis, there is no limit as how much money can be made by becoming one of these talented individuals!

Chapter 10

HOW TO RENT OUT YOUR CAR PARKING SPACE.

If you have a spare parking space in your garage or driveway, then it may be the perfect solution for renting out. A lot of people don't think about getting involved with this market, but it is actually very profitable and can provide you with some extra money to put towards other things.

The great thing about renting out your parking space is that it's incredibly flexible. You can rent out your parking space whenever you want and for as long as you want, which means that if you have guests who are coming over just for dinner or drinks and don't need their own car to get there, then they'll be able to use yours instead! You could also rent out the space when no one else has parked at all—in order to make extra money from people who don't live nearby.

If there were ever a time where we needed an extra resource in our lives (and there usually is), this would be it: someone else would pay us money so that we don't have to worry about finding somewhere else before they come back later on in the evening/early morning/whatever time frame works best for whoever comes over first thing tomorrow morning after sleeping through most of today's events...

It's a good idea to say in your advert how much space you have available, and what type of vehicle can fit in to give potential renters an idea of what they might be able to park.

This way they know if they want to rent from you or not before they contact you.

Come up with a name for your space.

You can use your name, or you can choose to go by a nickname that you and your friends would like to be called. Some people just say "the garage" or "the car park," but these aren't very imaginative names and don't provide much information about what the space is used for.

There are many ways to come up with a good description of your parking space:

- Use numbers (1-10) - This one is simple because everyone knows what numbers mean! If you're selling tickets online, this could be helpful if someone needs help remembering how many tickets have been sold in total. If there isn't enough room for everyone who buys tickets at once, then it would also be handy if people knew how many spaces they could take advantage off while they waited their turn at checkout counter register machine 2A3B4C5D6E7F8G9H0I1J2K3L4M5N6O7P8Q 9R0S1T2U3V4W5X6Y7Z8

Renting out your parking space is a great way to make extra cash. You can decide when you want to rent it out, and if you don't use it for a few days then the website will automatically send you an email asking if they can rent your space again.

The best part of renting out parking spaces is that they are flexible. This means that even if there is no demand for parking spots in town on certain nights or weekends, there still may be someone looking for one nearby so long as they know where it is!

If you're thinking about renting out your parking space, it's a good idea to do some research first. Find out what kind of car people are looking for and then come up with a name that will make them want to book the space. Your car should be easy to find too, so make sure its location is listed on the advert!

Chapter 11

HOW TO SELL YOUR HAIR FOR WIGS OR EXTENSIONS.

You've probably heard about people selling their hair for wigs and extensions, but you may not know that there are lots of ways to make money from your own hair. It's true - there are actually quite a few people out there who have done just that and made some good money doing so. If you're interested in selling your hair, I'll show you how!

You probably think you don't have the right hair for extensions, but you do!

Extensions are made from real human hair and usually have a keratin-based glue that holds them in place. This makes them strong enough to withstand daily wear and tear, which means they'll last longer than synthetic wigs or weaves. They also come in many different lengths and colors so there's no limit to what kind of look you can create with your extensions!

You need at least 8 inches of hair to sell, so wait until your hair is long enough. If you're getting a trim or cut, don't worry about it—if it looks good and feels good and you're not in any pain, then keep going!

However, if there are some parts that are too short (for example: bangs), then this will affect the quality of your wig or extension. In this case we recommend cutting those parts off before selling them on our website because they could easily get damaged when being sold by someone who doesn't know how to care for their own personal appearance properly."

Apply for listings that indicate the kind of hair they want.

If you want to sell your hair, it's important that you know what kind of hair they want. If a listing says "black" or "white," then it's likely that they don't want curly or straight. If someone posts an ad saying "long," then this means they want long-haired extensions in particular.

If there aren't any listings that specify the kind of hair they want, then sell your locks to a wig maker instead!

Ultimately, you will have to pay some money up front if you want to sell your hair. You'll need to pay for shipping and the cost of cutting and coloring it. The rest should go toward paying for the wig or extension that you choose.

You can give your hair a few cuts before you send it in. This is especially helpful if you want to shorten the length of the strands or leave them longer, and it gives the stylist more options for how to style them.

If this sounds like something that might be helpful for you and your budget, consider taking some time out of your day to give yourself a haircut before sending off those strands of hair!

You can also cut down on costs by using good quality scissors when doing so yourself (or getting someone else from home). There are many different types of scissors available at stores such as Walmart or Target that will help keep costs low while still giving great results!

You'll need to braid your hair and ship it off to get paid.

- You'll need to braid your hair and ship it off to get paid.
- If you're interested in selling your hair instead of donating it, consider selling it through a wig maker or hair extension company. These companies will take the

braid from you and sell the extensions on their own websites, then pay you for the sale (though they may not offer as much as what you'd get from a donation).

Don't worry too much about what kind of cut you're getting - just get one that feels good!

If your hair is long, don't worry about the length. Just get one that feels good and looks good.

If your hair is short, don't worry about the length either. We can always add more layers later if needed!

When getting a trim or a haircut, it might be helpful to ask your stylist this question instead.

- Can they cut your hair in a way that will make it easier to sell?
- Will they give you a haircut that will look good with extensions?
- Can they give you a haircut that looks good without wearing wigs/extensions at all times?

Hair color is not as important when it comes to selling your hair, but it still matters. Hair color can affect the price if you want to sell your hair online. If you have an unusual color or dye job, then buyers might be turned off by the idea of buying a wig made from someone else's head.

You should also consider what kind of texture your natural locks have and whether they're coarse or fine in appearance before making any decisions about how much money you should charge for this part of the purchase process (or even if there will be one at all).

There's money to be made selling your hair.

You can make money with your hair. It's a fact, but you may not be aware of it. The more you sell, the better it will be for you financially. If you have long enough hair and are willing to do some extra work for it, there's no reason why selling your hair shouldn't bring in some extra cash (like $1-2 per pound).

There are several ways to make money from selling your own strands:

- Your own wig or extension business - Make sure that any potential clients know exactly what they're paying for before doing anything else! This could also mean showing them how much time/effort goes into making each wig so that customers understand why this particular style isn't available elsewhere...and hopefully convince them not only how much effort went into making their new creation but also why they should buy one instead of going elsewhere; maybe even offer discounts on future orders if they decide now might be good timing after seeing what kind of quality work went into making this particular item?

- Hairpiece manufacturers - These companies often pay well over minimum wage because there are lots more workers needed than just those working directly together at specific times during production; therefore more money coming back into local economies where jobs exist outside major cities like New York City where most people live nowadays anyway--so having skilled workers around makes sense economically speaking even though many people wouldn't necessarily see them as being "skilled" due purely financial reasons alone."

That's all there is to it! As long as you're honest about what kind of cut you want, your stylist can help you find a great one that fits your lifestyle and budget.

Chapter 12

HOW TO BECOME A VIRTUAL ASSISTANT.

It's pretty easy to get started as a virtual assistant. The most important things you need are a workspace and the right tech set-up. It might be helpful to read our guide on how to start an online business, but if this is new to you check out our list of resources below!

1. Set up a workspace/office

Set up a workspace. Set up a virtual office.

2. Figure out your tech set-up

Once you've decided to start your own business, the first thing to do is figure out what equipment and software you need. The best way to do this is by reading up on the topic and making a list of must-have items that will help make your new venture successful.

Some important considerations include:

- What kind of computer do I need? Do I want something mobile or desktop? What type of RAM (Random Access Memory) should my system have in order for me to run all kinds? How much hard drive space does my

computer hold, how fast does it run at its highest setting, etc.?
- What software packages do I need on my computer? Unless it's an older program like Microsoft Office 2007 or 2010 then all versions are usually compatible with newer versions so there shouldn't be much trouble if someone else has installed them already onto theirs before purchasing one new set specifically tailored towards their needs."

3. Get the right tools

- You need a laptop. If you're going to be working from home, it's important that your computer is powerful enough to run the software and programs that will allow you to work remotely. Some businesses have specific requirements for their employees' computers; if yours does not meet those needs, then consider buying one specifically for virtual assistant use (or upgrading an existing one).
- You need an internet connection with enough bandwidth so that all of these programs can function smoothly and efficiently in real-time communication with clients over video calls or Skype meetings. This means having access both on-site at

home and off-site at work so as not only do they not have problems connecting with each other but also never lose connection during their daily duties because there isn't enough room within their office building where everyone could walk around freely without bumping into walls etc...

4. Get the right skills

- What skills do you need?

The first thing to do is to figure out what kind of work you want to do. This will help determine which skills are essential for your career path, and it will also help narrow down the field of potential employers. Many people choose to specialize in one or two areas—such as marketing or graphic design—and then find jobs that match those interests. Other people may have a more varied skill set, so they can apply their talents in a variety of fields. For example, someone might be an accomplished writer with excellent organizational skills; another person might have great computer programming ability but lack writing experience (or vice versa). Both types of individuals would be suitable virtual assistants because they'll have different strengths that employers need in order to achieve their goals efficiently and effectively.

- How do I improve my current skills?

There are many ways—both formalized ones like taking classes at schools or online resources such as Lynda (a subscription service provider) as well as informal ones through practice on your own time —that can help improve the way you think about tasks and solve problems efficiently.* How do I find mentors who can teach me new things? There are plenty of organizations out there offering free mentoring programs where professionals from different industries mentor young people interested in learning new skills related specifically towards becoming virtual assistants.* Where should I start looking for courses which teach how one learns faster than normal pace due mainly due its nature being interactive rather than passive listening which makes learning easier too since every second counts when trying something new thus making sure everything goes smoothly without any interruptions during class hours

5. Decide on your services and rates

Once you have a good idea of what your services are, it's time to decide on your rates. This will be a crucial step in the process of setting up your virtual assistant business. While it's important to charge enough for the quality of work and time spent, you also need to make sure that you're charging enough so that people hiring you are willing to pay them.

To set up pricing structures for different types of clients who need help with specific tasks or projects, look into sites like Upwork (formerly Odesk) or Freelancer where there are plenty of virtual assistants available who can help with everything from simple keyword research all the way up through complex website design projects!

6. Start advertising your business

- Start with a website. The first step in any business is to have an online presence, and it's the same for virtual assistants. You can create your own website, or you could use one that already exists.
- Build a list of potential clients by posting on social media sites like Facebook and LinkedIn, as well as through email marketing campaigns that focus on specific industries or geographic areas where you want to work. If you're looking for work as an assistant but don't know where to start—or are just starting out—this could help build up your reputation within certain circles of people who might hire someone like yourself in the future!

- Connect with other VAs on platforms like Meetup and Facebook groups (or whatever platform they use). These groups are great because they give people all over the world opportunities to connect with each other using common interests such as websites/businesses related towards technology-related fields such as web development; SEO experts; virtual assistants etcetera...

We have some step by step guide to help you build your virtual assistant company.

- Get a good workspace.
- Get the right tools.
- Get the right skills.
- Decide on your services and rates, then start advertising your business online, in newspapers and magazines etc., so that people can find out more about you and contact you when they need help with their projects or tasks!

We hope this article has helped you understand the process of becoming a virtual assistant. If you are ready to get started on building your own virtual assistant company, we have some step by step guide to help you build your virtual assistant company.

Chapter 13

HOW YOU CAN SELL YOUR USED BOOKS ON AMAZON.

If you're like me, you have a lot of books that are taking up space. You may even have tons of old textbooks that could be used for school projects or for second-hand book sales. The good news is that Amazon has made it easy to sell your used books on their site. There are some guidelines and tips to follow before selling on Amazon so that your item will be eligible for the best possible price.

How can I sell used books on amazon?

- Sign up for an Amazon seller account and add your used books to your inventory
- Set the selling price of each book, which can be set as low as $0.01 or higher than $100 per book depending on what you're willing to sell it for
- Select the shipping method you prefer (1-Day, 2-Day or Overnight) so that buyers can receive their items faster and in good condition
- Set up payment methods such as credit cards or electronic checks using PayPal

How much money you can get selling used books on Amazon?

How much money you can get from selling a book depends on the condition of the book. If it's in good condition, then you can sell more than one copy for $10 each. In fact, if you have a lot of books that are in good condition and want to sell them all at once, then this would be possible for sure!

But even though it may seem like there is no limit on how many copies an author will be able to sell their used books through Amazon Marketplace (the platform where authors sell their used books), we do have some rules:

- Only one person per household can have access to this service; otherwise they will be removed from our system immediately!

How do people get free books to sell on Amazon?

There are several ways to get free books, and you can use them whether you're selling your own used books or buying them from someone else.

- Buy Used Books: You can buy used books from thrift stores, garage sales and online bookstores. This is one of the most popular

ways to find free novels because it's easy and convenient for people who don't want to spend a lot of time searching for good deals on Amazon (or even if they do). All you need is an internet connection!
- Sell Your Own Stuff: If your home is getting cluttered with old junk from years past—and let's face it: We all have stuff we've accumulated over time—you might consider selling some of these items online instead! It'll save room in your house while simultaneously earning some extra revenue through Amazon's FBA program (that stands for "fulfilled by Amazon").

Where do you find free books to sell on Amazon?

There are many places you can find free books to sell on Amazon. Some of the most common include:

- Donate your books to charity. If you have a local library or school, they may be able to accept your library materials for their shelves and add them to their collection. You can also donate these items directly through the internet by visiting sites like Freecycle and Craigslist, where users post ads looking for others who want their unwanted goods

- (books included) removed from their homes or businesses.
- Ask family and friends if they would like one of your old textbooks/magazines instead of keeping it around as clutter! This may seem strange at first but I assure you that once someone has read something that wasn't theirs before then there's no reason not give it away too!

Are used book stores or Amazon better for selling books?

Amazon is a great place for selling used books because it has a huge audience. The store has been around for years, and it's one of the most popular sites on the web. Thousands of people visit Amazon every day looking for things to buy or sell.

This means that if you have a book that's in good condition but not quite perfect yet (like this copy of Harry Potter and the Philosopher's Stone), then selling it on Amazon will help make up some of the money needed to get yours fixed up!

What are some tips for selling used books on Amazon?

- Make sure you are selling the right book.

- Be specific with your title and description.
- Be honest about the condition of the book, and don't try to trick people into buying a "good" copy when it's really not up to snuff (the cover is torn or there's no dust jacket).
- Use a professional cover photo that accurately reflects how well-made your book actually is. This will help potential buyers see what they're getting before they buy, which can save them money on shipping costs as well!

You can make money by selling your old books.

There are many ways to make money. One of them is selling used books on Amazon.

If you have old books that you don't want anymore and no longer use, it's possible that they can bring in some extra cash. The most important thing when selling used books on Amazon is finding the right place for your products, because if they're not displayed properly or aren't high enough quality then no one will buy them from you!

The easiest way to sell anything (used or new) on Amazon is through their marketplace section called "Buy Box". When someone searches for something on their page and clicks "buy box", then this will show up above what other sellers have listed - so if there isn't anything in position 1 then people would click around looking for something else until finally seeing yours come up again at position 2!

You can make money by selling your old books.

Chapter 14

HOW TO CREATE A BLOG FOR FREE AND MAKE MONEY FROM IT.

Blogging is a great way to get your name out there, gain new followers and make money. But if you want to do it on the cheap or are just starting out, then you may be wondering how to create a blog for free. Well, let me tell you that it's possible! In this article I'm going to explain my process for making money from my blog as well as how other people have done it in the past.

Start a WordPress blog.

- WordPress is the most popular blogging platform in the world. It's very easy to use and has many free themes and plugins available for it, making it a good choice for beginner bloggers.
- You can start your own blog by installing WordPress on your web server or hosting provider's account with just one click of your mouse. The website will look like this: [link](https://wordpress.org/about/)
- Once you've installed WordPress, there are plenty of themes available from which you can choose one (or more) that matches your personal style! If you want something more

professional looking than what comes pre-installed with every new installation then I would recommend checking out these premium themes: [link](https://themeforest.net/category/wordpress-themes/)

Figure out what you're good at.

- Figure out what you're good at.
- Make a list of the things that are most interesting to you, and why they're interesting. If there is anything on this list that doesn't make sense (for example, "I like cats" or "I'm an expert at making friends"), then consider removing it from your blog for now until you have time to figure out how best to incorporate it into your content.
- Look for common themes in these lists and try brainstorming ways of using them into blog posts or other types of content on your site (if necessary!).

Pick a blogging platform.

There are many options for hosting your blog, but WordPress is by far the most popular. If you're just starting out and want to try out different platforms, search for "blogging platform" on Google and check out some of the results.

If you're looking for a free option, Tumblr is another popular choice (and it has its own share of drawbacks). Medium is also worth considering if you want an easier-to-use platform than WordPress or Tumblr.

Design your blog.

It is important to design your blog in a way that shows off your personality and style.

- Pick a theme that matches your niche. You need to have something that looks good on mobile, so choose a theme with responsive design options.
- Choose a theme that is easy to customize, but also looks good out of the box. If you want more control over how the site looks, then choose one of these templates: [ThemeForest](https://www.themeforest.net/) or [WordPress](http://codexbuilds.com/wordpress-themes/).
- Be sure all of your pages load quickly by using caching plugins like W3 Total Cache (https://wordpressbbpressoneofmyfavoriteblogsbloggingtutorialsandtips)-this will help speed up page load times by reducing server calls made by each page request!

Create your website.

To create your blog, you will need to choose a domain name and hosting provider. You can use any of the following options:

- A domain name of your choice (example: blogtothemes.com)
- A dedicated subdomain on one of our shared hosting plans (example: blogtothemes.wordpress.com)
- Your own custom hostname and IP address

Secure your domain name and web hosting.

If you haven't already, it's time to secure your domain name and web hosting. This can be done through a company like GoDaddy or HostGator, who will help you register the name of your blog on their server. If you're using WordPress as the content management system (CMS), then there are free options from Bluehost and Dreamhost that offer good security features for free with limited bandwidth limits—but these companies also come with additional costs if you want more than basic hosting capabilities (such as unlimited storage space or data transfer speeds). These services cost between $5-$10/month depending on what level of service is purchased; however most people don't need anything fancy so this shouldn't be an issue unless they want something like custom domains or high speed connections etc., which would require paying extra money each month over what's required by just having basic things set up correctly first time around!

Write great content.

The first step to creating a blog is to write great content. Great content is what makes readers want to come back and read more of your posts. It's important that you are writing about something that interests you, or else your readers will quickly lose interest in reading your blog.

If you're looking for ways on how to make money from blogging, then focus on topics related with what interests you most! You can also try making money through affiliate marketing (selling other people's products) so that when someone buys those products through one of the links in your article/blog post then it pays off for both parties involved in this transaction: seller gets commission fee while buyer receives discounted price due to referral program offered by company selling them product(s).

Build an email list and use it to generate revenue from your blog.

Email marketing is one of the most effective ways to build traffic and revenue. It's also a great way to grow your email list, which is your most important asset in this business.

In order to use your blog as an online course or product, you need an email list that can help generate revenue for you through affiliate marketing. An ideal subscriber will be interested in what you have written about on the blog and will be willing to buy something from you based on those insights.

There are several ways that you can generate income from paid advertising via email:

It is possible to start you own blog for free, and generate revenue from it using affiliate links and ads.

You can start your own blog for free, and generate revenue from it using affiliate links and ads.

You can use your blog to promote products and services you believe in, or even create your own products that you have created yourself. This is what we call "affiliate marketing", where the person who visits the site gets paid a commission when they buy something from an advertiser on their site.

You can also use affiliate marketing to promote products you have been paid to promote - like an e-book on how to build websites, or an eBook on how to make money online (which I've written).

It's not as hard as you might think. Start with a free WordPress blog, pick a blogging platform and design your site. Then, use affiliate links to generate revenue from your blog by selling products and services on it. Your readers will love what you have to say and when they need something done for them, they will turn to you first!

Chapter 15

HOW TO WRITE AN EBOOK AND SELL IT ONLINE.

Writing an ebook is a great way to make money, but it can be intimidating. You may be tempted to hire a ghostwriter or pay someone else to do the work for you. But if you know how to write your own book with these tips, then it doesn't take much time or money at all!

Do your homework

Before you start writing, it's important to do your homework. You can't just write an ebook and expect it to sell itself—you need to know what your competition is, what your customers want and how you can offer something unique that no one else does.

The first step in this process is knowing who your audience is and where they are located. If possible, access a list of keywords related to writing ebooks and see which ones come up most often when someone searches for "write my ebook" or similar terms on Google or Bing: these would be great places for potential titles! Once we've identified our target audience (and their interests), next comes research: find out about them by reading about their demographics, browsing through blogs written by those same people/groups of people (or even creating one yourself), etcetera ad nauseam until finally reaching peak saturation point where all remaining information has been exhausted...

Find your niche

It's important to find a niche that you are passionate about and can research. If the topic is too broad, it may not be as interesting to readers. For example, if you write about how to make money online from home in your free time, then people will assume that this is what everyone does and might not be interested in your book if it doesn't offer any new information or tips on how they can do so themselves.

On the other hand if someone writes an ebook on how to get rich quick by starting an online business with minimal effort (which isn't necessarily bad), then again many readers won't be interested because there's nothing new here for them at all!

Create your ebook

- Write about something you know or are interested in

- Write about a topic that is easy to understand. You want your readers to be able to pick up your book and read it without difficulty, so make sure your writing style is simple and clear. If you're not sure what kind of language would work best for this purpose, try using an approach that emphasizes emotion rather than intellect—for example: "I'm so glad I found out how much fun it is!" instead of "The results were surprising."
- Make sure your ebook is easy-to-read. Your goal here isn't just making money; it's also getting people interested enough in what you've written (and yourself) so they'll come back again later on down the line when they need more information! So make sure everything inside serves up value right away...

Choose a price

When you're choosing a price, it's important to consider what your ebook is worth. A good question to ask yourself is: "What do people who don't know me think my eBook is worth?"

It's also important to determine the market value of your product and make sure that it's competitive with similar products on Amazon (or any other platform). The best way I've found for doing this is by using Google Trends data, which can show how often certain keywords were searched over time. If there aren't many books related to what I'm writing about and I want my book out there as quickly as possible, then I'll go ahead and set it at $0.99 because then people won't see how much content there really is inside! However if most other books on Amazon are selling for around $4-$5 per copy then maybe try raising the price up from $0.99 so those customers won't feel like they're getting ripped off when buying one too - especially since some people might not even realize until after purchasing theirs anyways!

Write a sales letter and choose images that sell

A sales letter is an email—or even a letter if you prefer—that sells your product. It's what people receive when they click on your ebook link or download the free sample of your book.

If you haven't written one yet, it's time to get started! If a sales letter sounds intimidating, don't worry—I'll show you how easy it can be! First things first: What is a sales letter? A good example might be email newsletters from companies like Amazon that offer special deals and discounts on their products; these emails are designed so that people will want more information about each company's products (which makes them more likely to buy).

Choose the right format for your ebook

The next step is to decide on a format and make sure that it works on all devices. There are several different formats available, including ePub and Mobi. Each of these has its own pros and cons, but they all have one thing in common: they're compatible with each other so if you choose ePub as your format then your readers can read it on any device or reader that supports the eBook standard (which includes everything from iPhones to Kindles).

The most popular choice among writers today is undoubtedly Kindle Format 8 (KF8), which uses Amazon's proprietary KF8 format for creating eBooks compatible with Kindles, iPads, Android phones and tablets as well as PCs running Windows 7+. If your book doesn't need special formatting like audio files or video tutorials then this should be fine for you!

Give it away to build an email list

The second way to get people to buy your ebook is by giving it away for free. This is a great way to build an email list and promote other products, but be warned: if you give away too much of your content on the internet, it will quickly become difficult or impossible to make money off of either one.

If you want a free copy of the book and don't mind giving away an email address in return, Amazon offers this feature as part of their Kindle Direct Publishing program (KDP). If anyone buys one copy through KDP they'll get an autoresponder message that includes their name & email address. You can also use this method when selling on other platforms such as Smashwords or CreateSpace (both owned by Amazon).

Sell it on your own website or blog

You can sell your ebook on your own website or blog.

You can also sell it on Amazon Kindle Direct Publishing (KDP).

You should consider selling it on other platforms like Gumroad and Payhip.

Add your book to Amazon Kindle Direct Publishing (KDP)

- Add your book to Amazon Kindle Direct Publishing (KDP).
- KDP is the best way to publish your ebook. You will not have any problems with this step, it's free and easy to use!
- Great for marketing your ebook

Promote it, promote it, and then promote it some more

- Promote your ebook on social media
- Use email marketing to send out a newsletter about the book, and encourage people to sign up for it.
- Create a landing page for your ebook. If you've written a blog post or article related to your book, link it from there so that people can find out more information about it too! You can also include links in other posts (like Instagram stories) if they're relevant enough, but don't spam them with all sorts of irrelevant links just because they're available on Google search results pages...it'll make people feel like spamming is happening around everywhere which isn't what we want here at [insert name].

With these tips, you can write and sell your own ebook.

You've written your book, now it's time to sell it. Here are some tips on how to make that happen:

- Write the best book you can. This one is obvious but worth repeating—the more content you have, the better your chances of selling copies of your book are! Make sure that every chapter has at least 3-5 pages of text in it and make sure there is plenty of room for people who want more information on any given topic or industry trend. You can even include some graphics in order to give readers something visual while still allowing them access all of their information from other sources (iBooks).
- Find a niche marketing strategy that works for you and choose a price point that makes sense for potential buyers (see our previous article about pricing strategies here). If possible try writing several books so as not only increase sales but also keep up with demand which means less stress for both parties involved when trying new ideas out later down the road!

With these tips, you can write and sell your own ebook. The key is to take action! You can start by doing some research on what kind of book appeals to you. Once you have a concept in mind, look for an expert to help guide you through the process of creating an ebook from scratch.

About the Author

Evangelist Anthony Chinedu is the evangelist and the founder at the Rapture Ready Evangelistic Ministries, speaker and author, he is the author of the book titled, THE GREAT GLOBAL AWAKENING, a book self-published in 2017 and can be found on lulu.com and every other reputable online bookstore, He also authored another book titled "COVID 19 PANDEMIC: The People, The Government and The Church" he is also the CEO of his pet project known as Catch Them Young, a project meant to reach out to our teen agers with the gospel via their school exercise books and catch them young for God's kingdom, he's been around the ministry for some time now and has been used greatly by the Lord in interpreting the end time prophecies and preaching the end time messages and breaking of the enemy's strongholds. He lives in Lagos Nigeria with his wife and three daughters. He's been married for 7 years now.

www.ingramcontent.com/pod-product-compliance
Lightning Source LLC
Chambersburg PA
CBHW070257220526
45465CB00004B/1644